The Months of the
Republican Calendar Year
from the
FGB
With Useful Dates
for the French Genealogist
Second Edition

Anne Morddel

Suggested library cataloguing:

Morddel, Anne

The Months of the Republican Calendar Year from the FGB With Useful Dates for the French Genealogist, Second edition

Summary: Description of French rural life through the seasons using the months of the Republican calendar and following Eugène LeRoy's *l'Année Rustique en Périgord*.

[1. Calendars. 2. France - History. 3. LeRoy, Eugène.] I. Title

ISBN 979-10-96085-01-9

Table of Contents

Introduction

This booklet contains thirteen posts from the first seven years of "The French Genealogy Blog"[1] on the subject of French rural life through the seasons using the months of the Republican calendar and following Eugène LeRoy's *l'Année Rustique en Périgord*. It follows on our first publication "French Genealogy From Afar"[2], which explains the basics of French genealogy, including a section explaining the Republican Calendar, and without which this booklet may seem a bit confusing. It is our most sincere wish that you, Dear Reader, would find it of use in your search for your French ancestors.

Our 2014-2015 Calendar, which is no longer available, contained historically important dates of interest to the French genealogist. We have added those dates for each month to this booklet.

---

[1] http://french-genealogy.typepad.com/genealogie/

[2] Like this booklet, available from www.lulu.com/spotlight/morddel

Germinal

The French Republican Calendar was in effect from September, 1793, beginning with year two, to the end of December, 1805. We have written about it before and that post is given in Our Book. We explained the twelve months of thirty days each and their names being based on the weather and agricultural activities in the north of France. In order to eradicate the custom days being associated with saints, each day was associated with something to do with nature or agriculture. It was actually quite a beautiful and logical creation, but it did not stick and most of it -- especially the names of the days -- is forgotten now.

Yet, as much as the English love their countryside or the North Americans love their wilderness, France loves her farmers, and the Republican Calendar is evidence of that. The nineteenth century French novelist, Eugène Le Roy, wrote a charming book about nature's cycles through the year, using the Republican Calendar, *l'Année Rustique en Périgord*, which we would like to share with you from time to time.

The year begins with the Vernal Equinox and the month of *Germinal*, or germination, the time when seeds begin to sprout. It is a time, Le Roy writes, when all the trees of the hedges are in flower -- poplar, ash, elm, field maple, Damson plum. We note that it is also when the very French boxwood -- when not pruned, as it usually is -- flowers with a sweet and heavenly scent.

Le Roy tells of the peasant and his wife, who wears heavy canvas clothing, dig the soil around their grape vines. They gather the trimmed off vine shoots into a little bundle called a *javelou*, which will be used in the autumn to stir the batter for crêpes, then tossed into the fire to help warm the house. His stoic peasants of the Périgord "have a hard life but are healthy and strong". They eat well: chestnuts, fruits, walnuts, truffles. They feed red wheat to their pigs to fatten them and fry the bacon in walnut oil.

He then waxes unbelievably lyrical about the glories of the peasant-owner's life and the evils of great landownership, quoting Montesquieu at last : "It is not enough, in a good democracy, for the parcels of land owned to be equal; they must be small." Le Roy was a firm believer in the principles of the Revolution, specially that of equality, and one could write a small thesis on authors with similar convictions who clung to the Republican Calendar in one way or another. Zola's *Germinal* was not, after all, entitled *Germination*.

Coming back from politics to nature, Le Roy notes that the true sign of Spring's definitive arrival is the call of the cuckoo, which, by the way, one can still hear often in France (we read it is no longer so in Britain and cuckoos are confined to clocks in California). He ends with a local proverb about listening for the cuckoo's call, in the *Périgordin* dialect of Occitan:

Entre martz e abriü,
Saubrez si lou coucu
Es mort ou viü.

Any Occitan dictionary owners out there?

Germinal runs from the 20th or 21st of March to the 19th or 20th of April. Dates of interest during this time are:

- 24 March 1871 - The City Hall of Paris was burned, with all of its centuries of records.
- 26 March 1871 - The Paris *Commune* was declared.
- 28 March 1854 - The Crimean War began.
- 29 March 1945 - Marginal notes on deaths began to be added to birth registrations.
- 31 March 1547 - Henry II became king of France.
- 1 April 1803 - It became possible to change one's name by law.
- 7 April 1498 - Louis XII became king of France.
- 8 April 1927 - Dates of banns cease to be entered in marriage registrations.
- 9 April 1736 - Louis XV dictates the format of parish registrations and mandates that copies of them be given to the government.
- 13 April 1598 - The Edict of Nantes gives some religious freedoms to Protestants.
- 18 April 1886 - Marginal notes about divorces must be noted on marriage and birth registrations.

Floréal

Firstly, we apologize for being late with this post. Poor Typepad has been under assault, the target of one of those attacks that seem to be the Internet version of a swarm of seventeen-year locusts, or perhaps like a suffocating cloud of the lake flies that come off of Lake Victoria; in any case, the insects of the Internet causing trouble.[3] Our compliments to the Typepad staff who have worked so hard to restore service and our humble blog.

During the attack, *Floréal* commenced. The second month of the Republican calendar, named for the time of wildflowers bursting into tiny blooms. Le Roy's book tells us that now is when the nightingale begins to fill the dark hours with song:

Chante, rossignol, chante,
Toi qui as le coeur gai!

Pour moi je ne l'ai guère,
Mon amant m'a quitté
Pour un bouton de rose
Qui lui ai refusé!

Je voudrais que la rose
Fut encore le rosier,
Et puis que le rosier
Fut encore à planter!

This was a time when there may have been many newlyweds, for often country marriages were timed in order to take advantage of festivals and feasts, either Carnival or the springtime butchering of a fattened pig at the end of Lent. Newlyweds and all others would be doing their spring planting during *Floréal*: carrots, buckwheat, oats, beans, potatoes. Though religion was meant to be

---

[3] It is this very issue that prompted us to transfer our posts to these booklets!

banned by those who created the Republican calendar, most country folk felt better about their sowing if the local *curé* took a procession around the fields saying a prayer to ward off late frosts and hail. Le Roy insists that this was a custom even in Roman times, as were the crosses at the entry of each village.

So far as we can tell, the ceremonies are gone, both religious and Republican, but the planting goes on in the countryside. Everyone has prepared their *potager* and the shops are full of young vegetable plants for those who cannot be bothered with seeds. We have some arugula going in the window.

Perhaps your French ancestor handed down the rhyme about the last day of April, or mid-*Floréal*:

À la Saint-Robert, tout arbre est vert.

Which should hold true unless he or she emigrated to the southern hemisphere!

Floréal runs from the 19th or 20th of April to the 20th of May. Dates of interest during this time are:

- 21 April 1944 - Women were granted suffrage.
- 24 April 1815 - Louis XVIII becomes king of France.
- 1 May 1693 - *Notaires* must register with the government the contracts that they write.
- 2 May 1668 - The Treaty of Aix-la-Chappelle extends France's northern border.
- 3 May 1553 - The inheritance of land must be recorded.
- 10 May 1774 - Louis XVI becomes king of France.
- 14 May 1610 - Louis XIII becomes king of France.
- 14 May 1643 - Louis XIV becomes king of France.
- 15 May 1768 - France acquires Corsica.
- 18 May 1804 - The First Empire of France begins.

Prairial

The month of *Prairial* is upon us. Prairie has just about the same meaning in French as it has in English, though the prairie that goes on forever in all directions of North American understanding would engulf with terrifying voraciousness the hedge-bound meadow that is a French idea of a *prairie*.

Our guide to the year of Republican calendar month, Eugène Le Roy, devotes his entire chapter on *Prairial* to hay-making. As our little place in the country is so swamped in grasses at the moment that the roof is almost invisible, we can vouch for the veracity that informs this emphasis.

Your rural French ancestors would have seen the engagement of the reaper for a tiny fee. The following day, he would begin work at the very first hint of light, long before dawn. Swinging his scythe rhythmically, steadily, and with great strength, he would work his way across a field, cutting down everything that grew, producing a heady perfume of grasses and wildflowers. Le Roy spares a few sentences of pity for those with hay-fever and none of sympathy for the moles that create the hills that knock the scythe's swinging out of sync. (Apparently "you miserable mole-boy" was a vicious bit of name-calling once.)

Finishing by eleven in the morning, the reaper went to the farmhouse for his pay and for a bowl of soup. Soup being so associated with the peasantry that, even today, no French hostess would dream of serving it, ever, at a dinner party. However, it was all a reaper could expect and perhaps all his hosts had to offer. Soup consumed, the reaper went home to sleep. His work was done.

Then, the real work began. The entire family and all farm labourers went out to the field to rake the hay to dry. For days they had to rake it and turn it to dry it. When it was dry, they had to stack it. Hay poles had been erected in the field. Branches were laid down first, then the hay stacked as high as possible, men stacking it, while women, atop the stacks, stamped it down as firmly as possible. Le Roy states that it is a hard job for all but especially for the women, "*les pauvres diablesses*".

Rewards were odd in days of yore, to be sure. By the end of *Prairial* and of the hay-making, the fields would have been filled with glow worms (while we may still have tall grasses, modern practices and products have pretty much wiped out those pretties). The evening custom, Le Roy assures, was for young men to fill a maiden's hair with glow worms, which he seems to have found charming but which calls to our imagination the poor girl being turned into a greenish Medusa.

Prairial runs from the 20th of May to the 19th of June. Dates of interest during this time are:

- 23 May 1959 - The destruction of the registers of marriage bans is permitted.
- 30 May 1574 - Henry III becomes king of France.
- 7 June 1793 - The "Reign of Terror" begins.
- 18 June 1815 - Napoleon and France are defeated at the Battle of Waterloo.

Messidor

The month of *Messidor* takes its name from the Latin word for harvest. Eugène Le Roy describes the backbreaking labour in the hot sun that was the wheat harvest. Dreading summer rains or a hail storm that could destroy the crop, and thus their supply of bread for the year, people worked as hard and as fast as they could, bent double in the fields, their heads so low that they were breathing the mixed dust of earth and chaff.

But, Le Roy exults, *Messidor* is also the month for celebrating the anniversary of THE REVOLUTION. Heroism! Struggle! Nobility! Fiery change! Fireworks!

The French Revolution involved a hefty amount of destruction, and Le Roy tidily links this to the pre-Revolutionary festival of Saint Jean, which itself was a Christian festival draped over the pagan rites of Mid-Summer. Bonfires all round. For a couple of weeks or so, people no longer being fussy about the exact date, there have been village fêtes for Saint Jean, with evening bonfires, all over the country. The government allows these fires for just a few short weeks, just for these festivals, (though some people also use this permission to burn their garden rubbish).

Your French ancestors, if they lived in villages, would have gathered at the *place* in front of the church, everyone bringing wood and faggots to build the bonfire. On top of the wood would be added pine and juniper branches, then bunches of fennel and mint for their scent. When darkness fell, the church door would open and the *curé* would come out, say a prayer, light the fire and retreat back into the church, leaving the parishioners to revert completely to paganism and whoop and dance round their inferno.

Mid-Summer night is now overlaid with yet another festival. It seems that those in power must always put their imprint on certain human rituals that will be performed no matter what happens, for all time. In France, the twenty-first of June is now "*Fête de la Musique*", an all-night celebration of music. In Paris, not only will there be concerts indoors and out, but every bar will have a band or a singer. People will dance in the streets, even -- or perhaps especially -- those on strike. In towns and villages, there will be music and people will gather together. In the village close to where we are at the moment in the southwest, the grocer -- whose shop happens to face the church and the *place* -- will be serving drinks at tables placed in the road and his teenaged son will play the guitar.

All of France is celebrating the beginning of Summer tonight.

Messidor runs from the 19th of June to the 19th of July. Dates of interest during this time are:

- 22 June 1940 - The Fall of France in WWII.
- 25 June 1794 - The law creating Departmental Archives is passed.
- 7 July 1798 - The Quasi-War between France and the United States begins.
- 10 July 1559 - François II becomes king of France.
- 14 July 1789 - The Bastille prison in Paris is stormed by a mob and the French Revolution begins.

Thermidor

The Republican calendar name for this month, *Thermidor*, needs no explanation. Perhaps, this year however, it is mere nostalgia, for this has been one of those summers that is so rainy and cold that we have had a fire in the grate on a number of evenings. There have been occasional days of extraordinary surges of the thermometer to 45 C, and then the reversion to cold and rain.

After about four pages on the beauties of the song of the lark, Le Roy writes that this is the month of threshing. By hand. With a flail. In the hot sun. People beat the cut wheat to separate the grain from the chaff. Le Roy comments that it was particularly hard for the women, as they had to keep up with the pace of the men or risk getting whacked by another's flail if the rhythm were lost. He also moans about the suffocating dust that would fill the air, as well as one's mouth, nose and throat, and stick to any exposed skin. (In spite of his poetic descriptions of the rustic life, Le Roy goes on so much about irritants of dust and pollen that we suspect he may have suffered from a number of allergies himself.)

For us, no flailing, but it looks as if the hedges will be producing a bumper crop of sloes (*prunelles sauvages*) this year and we will be harvesting them this week and making sloe gin (*eau de vie*). Should you find yourselves near Périgueux this summer, stop by for a glass!

Thermidor runs from the 19th of July to the 18th or 19th of August. Dates of interest during this time are:

- 19 July 1870 - The Franco-Prussian War begins.
- 20 July 1808 - French Jewish families are required to select permanent surnames.
- 26 July 1830 - The July Revolution begins.
- 2 August 1589 - Henry IV becomes king of France.
- 10 August 1678 - France acquires Franche-Comté.
- 13 August 1532 - Brittany is united with France.
- 15 August 1684 - The Treaty of Ratisbon gives France more land in the north west.
- 17 August 1897 - Marginal notes about legitimation and marriage are required to be added to birth registrations.

Fructidor

Fructidor began last week, but it has rained as much as if it were *Pluviôse*. According to our own countryside record keeping (about which we may be a tad compulsive, having noted down weekly weather trends for the past twenty years) the last time we had such a sodden summer was in 1998. As then, it has been cold and rainy, with a few days of sunshine. The pumpkins and tomatoes will never ripen this year, but the fields, normally brown by now, remain gloriously green. Today, it is cold enough to warrant a fire, and soon, back to the city for *la rentrée* and the seriousness of autumn.

In a normal year, however, *Fructidor* is a time of ripeness all around: wild plums, blackberries, peaches, then grapes. The wildflowers are abundant and going quickly to seed. It is the time when your French ancestors made the last cut of alfalfa and got in another sowing of clover. According to Le Roy, it was a month of heavy consumption of chickens - especially those that would not survive another winter -- and, as the hardest work was done for a while, of heavy wine consumption.

There was but one job remaining for the summer: the tidying of the fields by gathering all of the sheaves and loading them onto carts to be taken away. The last sheaf, or *gerbe*, placed on the last cart was tied up with ribbons and flowers and was the central symbol of a magnificent meal in the garden, the *Gerbe-baude*, as Le Roy calls it. (It was called the *parcie* in the Berry region, the *bavajada* in Auvergne, the *passée d'août* in Normandy.)

He paints a nice picture of such plenitude in nature, shared by all, giving a sense of *égalité*. Yet it was not so, for the custom of the festive meal at the gathering of the last sheaf was a share-croppers' celebration, coming after they had paid from their harvests their rents and dues and tithes to their lords and landlords and to the king. Then, they could divide the paltry remains and have a little party. If you have found, on an ancestor's marriage registration, that he was a *métayer*, then he was a share-cropper, and would have celebrated the end of summer's work thus.

Fructidor runs from the 18th or 19th of August to the 23rd of September. Dates of interest during this time are:

- 21 August 1791 - The Haitian Revolution begins in what was then Saint Domingue.
- 21 August 1791 - A map showing every town in France - *le cadastre napoleonien* is mandated.
- 23 August 1572 - St. Bartholomew's Day massacre of Protestants by Catholics.
- 25 August 1539 - The *Ordonnance de Villers-Cotterêts* requires that parishes begin to record births, marriages and burials.
- 30 August 1798 - marriages are required to take place in the town that is the seat of each canton. (The law was abolished two years later.)
- September 1921 - The first French identity card is issued.
- 1 September 1715 - Louis XV becomes king of France.
- 4 September 1870 - The Third Republic begins
- 5 September 1798 - Military conscription is established
- 12 September 1790 - The National Archives of France are created.
- 21 September 1792 - France becomes a republic.
- 22 September 1664 - Protestant parish registrations must be given to the government.

Vendémiaire

Autumn really is the most extraordinary season in France, a time of tender beauty and glorious harvests. In the Republican calendar, there are some "supplementary days" at about this time of year, to keep things on track with a sun that does not choose to follow the rigidity of mathematical perfection, and then begins the month of *Vendémiaire*. Eugène Le Roy, in his *Année Rustique en Périgord* began his chapter on *Vendémiaire*, naturally, with the grape harvest and all of the preparations for it.

Friends, neighbours, relatives from afar worked together, chatting and picking the grapes. In the shade of a willow the wine casks were set on the ground. People dumped in their grapes and were helped by a man wielding a chestnut branch to scrape their baskets clean. Flies and wasps joined in with orgiastic abandon, which Le Roy found charming, along with the reddened arms of the grape-scraper, "a rustic god".

At midday, everyone sat on the grass and, with their trusty pocket knives (surely Opinel) hacked into a crust of bread. Omelets appeared, as did goat's cheese, fresh walnuts and crêpes. And wine. In the evening, soup was the fare and each person who helped received a basket of grapes.

He lamented that the joys of country living were no longer popular. Everyone wanted to go to the beach. The wonderful type of harvesting that he described was disappearing; modern people "disdained rustic amusements and harvest festivals". His nostalgia is sincere; had he witnessed globalization, he would have despaired, and certainly joined José Bové.

The "neo-peasant" was perverted, knew nothing and had no love for the land. He also was less virile and fat. What happened to these new peasants? Some will become *journaliers* or *manoeuvres* (both words meaning day labourers) and "live in poverty". Some will go to the cities and disappear in the dregs of Society. Others will be recruited by agents to cross the Atlantic. One saw them on the quays at the ports, sitting on their pathetic baggage. Sad mothers and somber fathers wait, surrounded by their confused children, all "future victims of acclimatization".

Interesting to observe the immigration myths from the point of view of those who did not budge, *non*?

Vendémiaire runs from the 23rd of September to the 23rd of October. Dates of interest during this time are:

- 2 October 1795 - Internal passports are required.
- 4 October 1958 - The Fifth Republic begin.
- 13 October 1946 - The Fourth Republic begins.
- 22 October 1685 - The Revocation of the Edict of Nantes makes the Protestant religion illegal again.
- 22 October 1955 - Identity cards are required for all citizens.

Brumaire

Brumaire takes its name from *brume* - that morning mist that covers the dales when the autumn air is cooler than the earth. Le Roy writes of the rural life during *Brumaire* as it may have been for your French ancestors: the farmer's voice, calling to his oxen as he plows early in the morning, muffled by the mist and seeming to come from everywhere and nowhere at once; at mid-morning, the mist finally clears and beasts are allowed a rest "with their noses in the hedge"; when the fields are plowed, he sows the wheat, taking the seeds from a bag on his shoulder and flinging them in an arc while, behind him, all the family rake and cover them. This sowing was to have been done between the days of Saint-Michel (29 September) and Sainte-Catherine (25 November).

It is also the season for harvesting chestnuts and walnuts. Our friend, *Madame S.* told us of autumn crafts in school when she was a child. These included sticking matchsticks into fresh chestnuts to make animals and people, which sounds significantly more charming than our own childhood version of vegetable creatures: Mr. Potato Head. Currently, in the local agricultural cooperatives, the traditional walnut gathering tools -- an oval basket that rolls on the end of a pole -- still sells, and at a shockingly high price. Most people nowadays, however, use a tractor, as in the photo above, and one can see the result, both in the size of the harvest and of the harvester.

After autumn storms, there may come a time of warmth and sunshine; what folks in North America called an "Indian Summer" was the *été de la Saint-Martin* (11 November, remembered more now for being the date on which the Armistice ending World War I was signed) "the last smile from nature as the year decline". Saint Martin's Day also marks the beginning of fattening the pigs for Carnival - *"Pour chaque porc vient de la Saint-Martin."* This is followed by a graphic and poetic account of pig-slaughtering and sausage-making which we, as a vegetarian, choose to ignore, but which Le Roy, and most likely your French ancestors, found picturesque.

It was and is so popular throughout France that your family's traditional recipe could lead to identifying the region where your ancestors originated, should it not be known to you. Does one of these sausages, or *saucisses*, sound familiar to you?

- The *diot*, with nutmeg, is made in Savoy.
- The *gendarme*, from Vosges, mixes beef with pork and is smoked; it is always presented in two sections.
- The *saucisse de Montbéliard*, land of watchmakers, is also smoked and contains cumin.
- The *saucisse de Morteau*, from Franche-Comté, is a squat item and fatty. A grand peculiarity: when even more fat is added, it is called *Jésus*.
- The *saucisse de foie*, made exclusively from the pig's liver, is a treat from Ariège.
- The *knack*, made from beef, veal and pork, comes from Alsace and looks like a classic, American-style hot-dog (though too short for the ball-park version).

We will now go munch some fresh walnuts and have a glass of Bordeaux and ponder the sad fate of pigs.

Brumaire runs from the 23rd of October to the 21st of November. Dates of interest during this time are:

- 24 October 1648 - The Peace of Westphalia ends the Thirty Years' War.
- 26 October 1796 - The Departmental Archives are created by law.
- 27 October 1940 - The Vichy government requires identity cards.
- 28 October 1922 - Birth registrations must include the date and place of birth of both parents.
- 1 November 1954 - The Algerian War begins.
- 2 November 1795 - The Directory takes control of France.
- 9 November 1799 - The Consulate governs France.
- 11 November 1918 - World War I ends; Alsace-Lorraine is returned to France.
- 18 November 1738 - The Treaty of Vienna gives Lorraine to France.
- 20 November 1541 - Calvin mandates that Protestant baptisms shall be recorded.

Frimaire

Continuing with our study of the Republican Calendar's months, guided by Eugène Le Roy, we are now entering *Frimaire,* the month that takes its name from the French word for frost. It is a time of bitterly cold winds rattling dry leaves that cling to branches. Flowers have disappeared until, later in the month, the hellebores bloom. The long rows of cranes pass overhead on their way south. All is grey, bleak and cold.

Or it was, before global warming. This year, autumn has been glorious, golden, warm, sunny and bright. Paris feels like Phoenix; Dordogne feels like Dorset in May. Long ago, at this time of year, your French ancestors would be dining on thin soup, gathering sticks and broken branches for the fire, pruning trees with numb fingers. Were they to have had a *Frimaire* such as this year, they would have been astonished, for the combination of dampness from the odd bit of rain and so much warmth has produced a bonanza of mushrooms.

Last week, and utterly out of season, we were presented with a friend's surplus of *cèpes.* This week, we were wandering a field and came across a fairy ring of *faux-mousserons,* of which we harvested a few dozen.

Omelets! Soups! Stews! Plates full of mushrooms cooked in butter! Your French ancestors then would have been, as are your distant cousins today, giddy with gastronomical glee.

Le Roy wrote also of *Frimaire* being the time when the peasant hunter (e.g. poacher) was prowling around looking for chestnut shells cut in half, the sign of the hare. Apparently, he would sneak his bloody kill home underneath his coat. He kept well in the brush, where it was harder for patrolling *gendarmes* on horseback to pursue him though, if they did go after him, he ditched both gun and corpse under a stone and ran for it. If caught, he was fined but, as he usually was too poor to pay the fine, it was waived and he was released. Whereupon he retrieved his gun and the probably quite high hare and carried on poaching.

This romanticizing of the poor continues in France today. Everyone pities "the poor" so much that, when someone who has no money breaks the law, a charitably blind eye is turned. Fines are waived, rent need not be paid, no tenant -- however remiss with the rent -- may be evicted during the cold months (will that change with global warming eliminating cold months, we wonder). The attitude is very *ancien régime*, the only difference being that what was once an attitude of the rich is now the law. Under the veil of charity is the absolute determination to keep people in poverty and to discourage and block their efforts to improve their lot. From our observation, the French "protection" of the poor is really quite crushing and cruel.

Le Roy completes his chapter on *Frimaire* with much more discussion of poachers' "rights" (we paraphrase): "The peasant hunter feels he has hunting rights by reason of his poverty and is indifferent or even hostile to all economic considerations and to the bourgeois theories on species conservation." Being both vegetarian and an environmentalist, we hold no truck with such specious reasoning.

These lovely and not so lovely traditions may not last. Perhaps next year's month of frost will see us all at the beach.

Frimaire runs from the 21st of November to the 22nd of December. Dates of interest during this time are:

- 27 November 1838 - Pastry War with Mexico begins.
- 2 December 1851 - Napoleon III becomes Emperor of the Second Empire after a coup.
- 5 December 1560 - Charles IX becomes king of France
- 8 December 1861 - France's Mexican Adventure begins.
- 9 December 1905 - Church and State are separated by law in France.
- 13 December 1799 - Electoral lists are established
- 19 December 1946 - The Indochina War begins.
- 20 December 1848 - The Second Republic begins.

Nivôse

We are well and truly deep in the Republican Calendar month of *Nivôse*, which Le Roy introduces with this rhyme:

L'hiver n'est pas bâtard,
S'il ne vient tôt il vient tard.

Snow, ice, lead-coloured skies full of crows with cries like hawkers. It is a time when, long ago, your French ancestors would have stayed indoors and worked on the baskets, wooden cages, mole traps and flails needed in the spring and summer to come. Those who were poorer would have huddled together in dark stone houses around a fire that had just a few chips of wood to burn. The old ones, Le Roy tells, peeled and ate chestnuts while telling creepy stories.

Their lives were extremely hard at this time of year, especially if they were *journaliers* (day-labourers). They were paid only for the days that they worked and, in a season of bad weather, they did not work many days. Working days were further reduced by the many holy days and Sundays in winter. They suffered privation and hunger and often went into debt to feed their families.

On certain days, the wealthy invited the poor to their yards to receive gifts of bread. Le Roy rages against such charity.

"It is not hand-outs that they need. Pay them better wages!"

But winter is also the traditional time of the new year, which:

arrives dressed in white, like the queens of France.

We wish you all, Dear Readers, a very Happy New Year and we hope that 2015 will be a year filled with goodness.

Nivôse runs from the 22nd of December to the 21st of January. Dates of interest during this time are:

- 1 January 1515 - François I becomes king of France.
- 3 January 1979 - Terms of access to French archives are established.
- 9 January 1872 - Citizens of Alsace-Lorraine had to opt to remain French.
- 17 January 1806 - The voting age is lowered from 21 to 20.

Pluviôse

Though we have been having glorious blue skies this week, this is usually a time of rain, rain, rain; *il pleut, il pleut, il pleut*, hence *Pluviôse* in the Republican Calendar. Le Roy writes that this is a time when ponds are full of dirty water, farmers' fields are like swamps and everything that could do so is rusting. Then he goes on another of his rants against the *ancien régime*, that terrible time of despotic kings -- surely, he and Mark Twain would have hit it off?

Rarely, in his fury at the sufferings of the peasants before the Revolution, does Le Roy show any humour, but in writing about the cruel and spendthrift string of kings named Louis, he shares a rebus popular during the reign of Louis XIV against his Finance Minister, Colbert. We found it rather fun and share it here:

Venance	France	fer	Colbert
G	de la	K	la France

Which works out to say: "*J'ai souvenance de la souffrance qu'a souffert la France sous Colbert.*" Pity that the words "beneath", "below", "under", etc. do not make for such clever games in English.

Less playful but more valuable for understanding why your French ancestor may have been so keen to leave are Le Roy's discussions of the many famines France endured. He quotes a monk who counted forty-eight times of famine during a period of seventy-eight years prior to the Norman invasion of England. Think what more bread in Normandy might have meant to British history!

Famines (*disettes*) in France during the eighteenth century occurred in:

- 1709 - a year of a bitter winter
- 1729 - a famine lasting two years when the price of bread reached nine sous per pound thanks to grain speculators
- 1740-1742 - a famine that was felt across Europe as crops failed. Four hundred thousand people died in Ireland; Sweden lost twelve per cent of her population; the Seine flooded Paris, and thousands of French died of hunger, but this seems hardly to have been the French king's fault though his decision to allow grain speculation to continue was certainly odious
- 1745
- 1750 - a particularly bad famine in the southwest of France
- 1767-1768
- 1775-1776 - a couple of hard winters brought crop failures in some parts of the country, while other parts had perfectly normal weather. For this time of suffering and starvation, the entire court got in on the grain speculation lark. Queen, princes, clergy, ministers, all delighted in scooping some cash while people starved. Epidemics of typhus and dysentery followed
- 1784
- 1789 - and we all know about the cake story and what happened next

It would seem that the eighteenth century was a time to get out of France and if your ancestors were among those who did, we do hope they found enough to eat in their new home. We cannot help but wonder if any of them ever went in for grain speculation.

Pluviôse runs from the 21st of January to the 19th of February. Dates of interest during this time are:

- 10 February 1763 - End of the Seven Years' War sees France lose many colonial possessions.
- 15 February 1794 - The modern French flag is created.

Ventôse

Depending on the year, the month of *Ventôse* began on the 19th or 20th or 21st of February. Eugène Le Roy, whose work, *L'Année Rustique en Périgord*, we have been quoting in our series on the months of the Republican Calendar, gives a few paragraphs to descriptions of the wind howling through peasants' homes, down their chimneys (and, we might add, blinding with smoke the grannies cooking there), in through all the cracks in the wall, tearing slates from roofs and sending them whipping murderously though the air (well, actually, he says that they float "like feathers", but we have seen them fly like flung tomahawks). This writing of wind and fragile homes calls to our mind the times when we have watched on French television a news report of some hurricane or other in the Americas; French observers in the room always shake their heads like the Third Little Pig and invariably say "Americans always build their houses out of wood." Stone is the thing, you see.

Le Roy tells that your French farming ancestor would have begun planting alfalfa, oats and clover during *Ventôse*, and then......Carnival! Forget those Republican rules on religion and its festivals, *Mardi-gras* is the time when dispersed families reunite at the "paternal home" and party. Apparently, these celebrations brought forth unforgivable sneering from those "bourgeois who have two meals a day AND eat both with a fork". What do they know of the struggling peasants' rare opportunity to have a bit extra on the table? He then waxes lyrical once again on the noble, ever-suffering French peasant.

With this month of *Ventôse*, Le Roy ends his year, but not his book. Throughout, he has praised his peasant and the virtues of the agrarian life. His last chapter, *Sans-Culottides*, (originally those days that did not quite fit into the calendar but later a particularly radical group of peasantry during the Revolutionary years) sums up his, and the Revolution's manifesto:

- No one should own more land than he and those living under his roof can farm themselves.

- Everyone has the right to enough land to feed himself and those living under his roof.

He goes on to say that accumulation, capitalism, speculation and usury are all the activities of those that should be hunted, trapped or poisoned like animals (*espèces nuisibles*). His fury against those with large estates is boundless.

Thanks to Le Roy, we understand France a bit more.

Ventôse runs from the 19th of February to the 21st of March. Dates of interest during this time are:

- 23 February 1848 - The February Revolution begins.
- 26 February 1708 - A declaration of pregnancy is required from every unmarried or widowed woman - on pain of death.
- 5 March 1848 - Universal male suffrage is granted.
- 10 March 1818 - Military conscription is re-established.
- 14 March 1928 - It is required that *notaires* send their archives to the National or Departmental Archives.
- 18 March 1877 - The family book, or *livret de famille*, becomes a required document.

German and Dutch Names for the Republican Months

For those researching the civil registrations for their ancestors in German-speaking towns within France during the years when the Republican Calendar was in effect (1792-1806), understanding the months can be a bit of torture. So, we thought to share this nifty translated list that we have found:

- **Republican Calendar**   **German month name**
- Vendémiaire   Weinmonat
- Brumaire   Nebelmonat
- Frimaire   Reifmonat
- Nivôse   Schneemonat
- Pluviôse   Regenmonat
- Ventôse   Windmonat
- Germinal   Keimmonat
- Floréal   Blütenmonat
- Prairial   Weisenmonat
- Messidor   Erntemonat
- Thermidor   Hitzemonat
- Fructidor   Fruchtmonat

En plus:

FGB Reader, *Monsieur* V has very kindly sent this:
Here are the names for your Dutch readers:

Autumn: Wijnmaand, Mistmaand, Koudemaand
Winter: Sneeuwmaand, Regenmaand, Windmaand
Spring: Kiemmaand, Bloemmaand. Weidemaand
Summer: Oogstmaand, Hittemaand, Fruitmaand

9 791096 085019